Anti-Social Behaviour

Fergus Smith
B.Sc.(Hons), M.A., C.Q.S.W., D.M.S., Dip.M

in consultation with

Paul Carr
M.A. (Cantab)
District Judge (Magistrates' Courts)

Children Act Enterprises Ltd (CAE)
103 Mayfield Road
South Croydon
Surrey CR2 0BH

www.caeuk.org

© Fergus Smith 2004

British Library Cataloguing in Publication Data
A catalogue record for this book is available from the
British Library

ISBN 1 899986 81 2

Designed and typeset by Andrew Haig & Associates
Printed in the UK by The Lavenham Press

CAE is an independent organisation which publishes
guides to family and criminal law and provides
consultancy, research, training and independent
investigation services to the public, private and voluntary
sectors.

Contents

Abbreviations

ASBA 2003	Anti-social Behaviour Act 2003
ATCSA 2001	Anti-terrorism, Crime and Security Act 2001
CA 1989	Children Act 1989
CDA 1971	Criminal Damage Act 1971
CDA 1998	Crime and Disorder Act 1998
CJA 1991	Criminal Justice Act 1991
CJA 2003	Criminal Justice Act 2003
CJCSA 2000	Criminal Justice and Court Services Act 2000
CJPA 2001	Criminal Justice and Police Act 2001
CJPOA 1994	Criminal Justice and Public Order Act 1994
CSA 1997	Crime (Sentences) Act 1997
CYPA 1933	Children and Young Persons Act 1933
CYPA 1969	Children and Young Persons Act 1969
EA 1996	Education Act 1996
FA	Firearms Act 1968
HA 1996	Housing Act 1996
MHA 1983	Mental Health Act 1983

MPA 1839	Metropolitan Police Act 1839
NA 1996	Noise Act 1996
PACE 1984	Police and Criminal Evidence Act 1984
PCCSA 2000	Powers of Criminal Courts (Sentencing) Act 2000
PHA 1997	Protection from Harassment Act 1997
POA 1986	Public Order Act 1986
CJPA 2001	Criminal Justice and Police Act 2001
PRA 2002	Police Reform Act 2002
SOA 2003	Sexual Offence Act 2003
TCPA	Town and Country Planning Act 1990
TA 2000	Terrorism Act 2000
YJCEA 1999	Youth Justice and Criminal Evidence Act 1999

—

Introduction

■ This guide is for use by those in England and Wales who have a professional interest in 'anti-social behaviour' of children, young people or their families e.g. social workers, police or probation officers, teachers, health and housing professionals, community workers and solicitors.

■ It aims to provide easy access to and reinforce understanding of relevant provisions in:

- Anti-social Behaviour Act 2003
- Other Acts as cited

■ A subject index has been included so that a specific subject e.g. graffiti or alcohol may be looked up.

■ This guide should be used to supplement or reinforce, not replace reference to legislation itself, associated regulations or official guidance.

NB. Unless otherwise indicated, all legislation cited is now in force.

References are made throughout to other CAE guides which can provide further details of specified law.

Context

- In March 2003, following previous consultations, the government published a White Paper 'Respect and Responsibility – Taking a Stand Against Anti-Social Behaviour'.

- In October 2003, the government's action plan entitled 'Together: Tackling Anti-Social Behaviour' was initiated and set out what was described as an ambitious programme for improving the quality of life in communities.

- Alongside the above action plan and consequent increases in funding for Crime and Disorder Reduction Partnerships, the 'Together Actionline' and 'Together Academy' were launched. These are intended to provide practitioners with the training, advice and support they need.

- In January 2004, the Anti-social Behaviour Act 2003 received Royal Assent. This Act contains measures drawn up from across 5 government departments and builds on existing legislation to clarify, streamline and reinforce the powers that are available.

Part 1: Premises Where Drugs Used Unlawfully

Closure Notice [s.1 ASBA 2003]

■ A 'Closure Notice' becomes possible if a police officer of at least superintendent rank (known as the authorising officer) has reasonable grounds for believing that:

■ At any time during the relevant period (i.e. 3 months ending with the day on which s/he considers whether to authorise the issue of a closure notice) the premises have been used in connection with the unlawful use, production or supply of a Class A controlled drug, and

■ The use of the premises is associated with the occurrence of disorder or serious nuisance to members of the public [s.1(1);(10) ASBA 2003]

■ The authorising officer may authorise the issue of a closure notice in respect of premises if satisfied that:

■ The local authority for the area in which the premises are situated has been consulted

■ Reasonable steps have been taken to establish the identity of any person who lives on the premises or who has control of or responsibility for or an interest in the premises [s.1(2) ASBA 2003]

NB. Authorisation may be given orally or writing, but if given orally the authorising officer must confirm it in writing as soon as it is practicable [s.1 (3) ASBA 2003].

- A Closure Notice (which must be served by a constable) must [s.1(4);(5) ASBA 2003] :

  - Give notice that an application will be made under s.2 for the closure of the premises
  - State that access to the premises by any person other than a person who habitually resides in the premises or the owner is prohibited
  - Specify the date and time when and the place at which the application will be heard
  - Explain the effects of an order made in pursuance of s.2
  - State that failure to comply with the notice amounts to an offence
  - Give information about relevant service advice providers (defined by s.1(11) as information about names and means of contacting persons and organisations in the area that provide advice about housing and legal matters)

- Service of a Closure Notice is effected by:

  - Fixing a copy of the notice to at least 1 prominent place on the premises
  - Fixing a copy of the notice to each normal means of access to the premises
  - Fixing a copy of the notice to any outbuildings which appear to the constable to be used with or as part of the premises
  - Giving a copy of the notice to at least one person who appears to the constable to have control or responsibility for the premises and

- Giving a copy of the notice to any person who lives on the premises or who has control of or responsibility for or an interest in the premises or to any other person appearing to the constable to be a person of that description

■ The Closure Notice must also be served on any person who occupies any other part of the building or other structure in which the premises are situated if the constable reasonably believes at the time of serving the notice, that the person's access to the other part of the building or structure will be impeded if a Closure Order is made under s.2 ASBA 2003 [s. 1(7) ASBA 2003]

NB. It is immaterial whether any person has been convicted of an offence relating to the use, production or supply of a controlled drug [s.1 (8) ASBA 2003].

Closure Order [s.2 ASBA 2003]

■ If a Closure Notice has been issued under s.1, a constable must apply under s.2 to a magistrates' court for the making of a Closure Order [s.2(1) ASBA 2003] and the application must be heard not later than 48 hours after the notice was served in pursuance of s.1(6)(a) [s.2(2) ASBA 2003]

■ The magistrates' court may make a Closure Order if and only if it is satisfied that each of the following applies:

 • The premises in respect of which the Closure Notice was issued have been used in connection with the unlawful use, production or supply of a Class A controlled drug
 • The use of the premises is associated with the occurrence of disorder or serious nuisance to members of the public
 • The making of the order is necessary to prevent the occurrence of such disorder or serious nuisance for the period specified in the order [s.2(3) ASBA 2003]

■ A Closure Order is an order that the premises in respect of which the order is made, are closed to all persons for a period not exceeding 3 months, as the court decides, but the order may include such provision as the court thinks appropriate relating to access to any part of the building or structure of which the premises form part [s.2 (4); (5) ASBA 2003].

- The court may adjourn the hearing on the application for period of not more than 14 days to allow any of the following persons to show why a Closure Order should not be made:

  - The occupier of the premises
  - The person who has control of or responsibility for the premises
  - Any other person with an interest in the premises [s.2(6) ASBA 2003]

  NB. If the magistrates' court adjourns the hearing under s.2 (6), it may order that the Closure Notice continues in effect until the end of the period of the adjournment [s.2 (7) ASBA 2003].

Closure Order: Enforcement [s.3 ASBA 2003]

- If a magistrates' court makes an order under s.2, a constable or an authorised person may:

  - Enter the premises in respect of which an order is made
  - Do anything reasonably necessary to secure the premises against entry by any person [s.3(1);(2) ASBA 2003]

  NB. A person acting under s.2 may use reasonable force [s.3 (3) ASBA 2003].

- A constable or authorised person seeking to enter the premises to enforce a Closure Order must, if required to do so by or on behalf of the owner, occupier or other person in charge of the premises, produce evidence of her/his identity and authority before entering [s.3(4) ASBA 2003].

NB. A constable or authorised person may also enter the premises at any time while the order has effect for the purpose of carrying out essential maintenance of or repairs to the premises [s.3(5) ASBA 2003].

Closure of Premises: Offences [s.4 ASBA 2003]

■ A person commits an offence if s/he remains on or enters premises in contravention of a Closure Notice [s.4 (1) ASBA 2003].

■ A person also commits an offence if s/he:

  • Obstructs a constable or an authorised person serving a Closure Notice or enforcing a Closure Order
  • Remains on the premises in respect of which a Closure Order has been made or
  • Enters the premises [s.4(2) ASBA 2003]

■ A person guilty of an offence under s.4 is liable on summary conviction to imprisonment for period not exceeding 6 months, a fine not exceeding level 5 on the standard scale or to both [s.4(3) ASBA 2003]

NB. A person does not commit an offence under s.4(1) or s.4 (2) (b) or (c) if s/he has reasonable excuse for entering/being on the premises [s.4(4) ASBA 2003].

Extension and Discharge of Closure Order [s.5 ASBA 2003]

■ At any time before the end of the period for which a Closure Notice is made or extended, a constable may make a complaint to an appropriate JP for an extension or further extension of the period for which it has effect [s.5(1) ASBA 2003]

■ Such a complaint may not be made unless authorised by a police officer of superintendent rank or above who:

- Has reasonable grounds for believing that it is necessary to extend the period for which the Closure Order has effect, for the purpose of preventing the occurrence of disorder or serious nuisance to members of the public and
- Is satisfied that the local authority has been consulted about the intention to make a complaint [s.5(2) ASBA 2003]

■ If a complaint is made to the JP under s.5(1), s/he may issue a summons directed to, and requiring the following person/s to appear before the magistrates' court so as to answer the complaint:

- The persons on whom the Closure Notice relating to the closed premises was served
- Any other person who appears to the JP to have an interest in the closed premises but on whom the Closure Notice was not served [s.5(3) ASBA 2003]

NB. If the court is satisfied that the order is necessary to prevent the occurrence of disorder or serious nuisance for a further period, it may extend the period for which the order has effect by a period not exceeding 3 months, though a Closure Order must not have effect for more than 6 months [s.5(4);(5) ASBA 2003].

- Any of the following persons may make a complaint to an appropriate JP for an order that a Closure Order is discharged:

  - A constable
  - The local authority
  - A person on whom the Closure Notice relating to the closed premises was served under s.1(6)(d) or (e) or s.1(7) ASBA 2003]
  - A person who has an interest in the closed premises but on whom the Closure Notice was not served [s.5(6) ASBA 2003]

- The court must not make an order discharging a Closure Order unless it is satisfied that it is no longer necessary to prevent the occurrence of disorder or serious nuisance to members of the public [s.5(8) ASBA 2003].

Appeals [s.6 ASBA 2003]

- An appeal against an order made under s. 2 or 5 ASBA 2003 or against a decision not to make an order under either of those sections must be brought to the Crown Court before the end of the 21st day following the court's order/decision [s.6 (1); (2)ASBA 2003].

- An appeal against an order under s.2 or s.5(4)may be brought by a person:

  - On whom the Closure Notice relating to the premises was served under s.1(6)(d) or (e)
  - Who has an interest in the closed premises but on whom the Closure Notice was not served [s.6(3) ASBA 2003]

- An appeal against the decision of a court not to make such an order may be brought by:

  - A constable
  - The local authority

  NB. On an appeal under s.6, the Crown Court may make such order as it thinks appropriate [s.6(5) ASBA 2003]

  Sections 8–10 address access to other premises, reimbursement of costs, and exemptions from liability for certain damages and compensation.

Part 2: Housing

Landlords' Policies and Procedures [s.12 ASBA 2003]

- S.12(1) ASBA 2003 inserts into the Housing Act 1996 a new s.218A applicable to a:
  - Local authority housing landlord
  - Housing action trust landlord
  - Registered social landlord

- The landlord must prepare and publish within 6 months of implementation of this section, a policy about, and procedures for dealing with occurrences of anti-social behaviour [s.218A(2);(3) HA 1996].

- The landlord must from time to time keep the policy and procedures under review and when thinks appropriate, publish a revised statement [s.218A (4) HA 1996].

- Copies of the above statement must be available for inspection at all reasonable times at the landlord's principal office and be provided on payment of a reasonable fee to anyone requesting it [s.218A(5) HA 1996]

- The landlord must also prepare a summary of its current policy and procedures and provide without charge, a copy of the summary to anyone who requests it [s.218A(6) HA1996]

NB. In preparing and reviewing the policy and procedures, the landlord must have regard to guidance issued by the Secretary of State in the case of the local authority or housing action trust and by the relevant authority under s.36 in the case of a registered social landlord [s.218A (7) HA 1996].

Injunctions Against Anti-social Behaviour on Application of Certain Social Landlords [s.13 ASBA 2003]

■ S.13 (1) ASBA 2003 inserts into the Housing Act 1996 new sections 153A–153E as follows.

Anti-social Behaviour Injunction [s.153A HA 1996]

■ S.153A(1) Housing Act 1996 applies to conduct which is capable of causing nuisance or annoyance to any person and which directly or indirectly relates to or affects the housing management functions of a relevant landlord.

■ The court on the application of a relevant landlord may grant an 'Anti-social Behaviour Injunction' if each of the following 2 conditions below is satisfied.

■ The first condition is that the person against whom the injunction is sought is engaging, has engaged or threatens to engage in conduct to which s.153A applies [s.153A(3) HA 1996]

■ That second condition is that the conduct is capable of causing nuisance or annoyance to any of the following:

  • A person with a right (of whatever description) to reside in or occupy housing accommodation owned or managed by the relevant landlord

- A person with a right (of whatever description) to reside in or occupy other housing accommodation in the neighbourhood of housing accommodation cited immediately above
- A person engaged in lawful activity in or in the neighbourhood of housing accommodation as described above
- A person employed (whether or not by the relevant landlord) in connection with the exercise of the relevant landlord's housing management functions [s.153A(4) HA 1996]

NB. It is immaterial where conduct to which s.153A applies, occurs [s.153A(5) HA 1996]

Injunction Against Unlawful Use of Premises Injunction [s.153B Housing Act 1996]

■ The court, on the application of the relevant landlord may grant an injunction prohibiting the person in respect of whom the injunction is granted, from engaging in conduct which consists of or involves using or threatening to use, housing accommodation owned or managed by a relevant landlord for an unlawful purpose [s.153B(1)&(2) HA 1996].

Injunctions: Exclusion Order and Power of Arrest [s.153C Housing Act 1996]

■ If the court grants in injunction under s.153A(2) or s.153B(2) and it thinks that the conduct consists of or includes the use or threatened use of violence, or that there is a significant risk of harm to a person mentioned in s.153A(4) above, it may:

- Include in its injunction, a provision prohibiting the person in respect of whom the injunction is granted, from entering or being in any premises or any area specified in the injunction [s.153C(1) & (2) HA 1996]

NB. The court may attach a power of arrest to any provisions of the injunction [s.153C (3) HA 1996].

Injunctions Against Breach of Tenancy Agreement [s.153D Housing Act 1996]

- S.153D applies if a relevant landlord applies for an injunction against a tenant in respect of the breach or anticipated breach of a tenancy agreement on the grounds that the tenant is:

  - Engaging or threatening to engage in conduct that is capable of causing nuisance or annoyance to any person, or
  - Allowing, inciting or encouraging any other person to engage or threaten to engage in such conduct [s.153D(1) HA 1996]

- The court may proceed under subsection (3) or (4) as described below if it is satisfied that:

  - The conduct includes the use or threatened use of violence, or
  - There is a significant risk of harm to any person [s.153D(2) HA 1996]

■ The court may include in the injunction a provision prohibiting the person in respect of whom it is granted from entering or being in any premises or area specified in the injunction [s.153D(3) HA 1996]

NB. The court may attach a power of arrest to any provision of the injunction [s.153D (4) HA 1996].

Injunctions: Supplementary [s.153E Housing Act 1996]

■ For the purpose of ss.153A–153D:

■ An injunction may be made for a specified period or until varied or discharged and/or have the effect of excluding a person from her/his normal place of residence [s.153E(1);(2) HA 1996]

- An injunction may be varied or discharged by the court on an application by:
- The person in respect of whom it is made
- The relevant landlord [s.153E(3) HA 1996]

NB. If the court thinks it just and convenient it may grant or vary an injunction without the respondent having been given such notice as is otherwise required by rules of court [s.153E (4) HA 1996], though it must give her/him an opportunity to make representations as soon as it is practicable for her/him to do so [s.153E (5) HA 1996].

■ A relevant landlord may be:

  • A housing action trust
  • A local authority (within the meaning of the Housing Act 1985)
  • A registered social landlord
  • (For the purposes of s.153D) a charitable housing trust which is not registered as a social landlord [s.153E(7); (8) HA 1996]

■ Housing accommodation includes:

  • Flats, lodging-houses and hostels
  • Any yard, garden, outhouses and appurtenances belonging to the accommodation or usually enjoyed with it
  • In relation to a neighbourhood, the whole of the housing accommodation owned or managed by a relevant landlord in the neighbourhood and any common areas used in connection with the accommodation [s.153E(9) HA 1996]

Security of Tenure: Anti-social Behaviour [s.14 ASBA 2003]

- S. 14 inserts a s.82A to the Housing Act 1985 **(demotion because of anti-social behaviour)** which applies to a **secure** tenancy if the landlord is:
  - A local housing authority
  - A housing action trust
  - A registered social landlord [s.82A(1) HA 1985]

- The landlord may apply to a county court for a Demotion Order which has the following effect:
  - The secure tenancy is terminated with effect from the date specified in the order
  - If the tenant remains in occupation of the dwelling house after that date a demoted tenancy is created with effect from that date
  - It is a term of the demoted tenancy that any arrears of rent payable at the termination of the secure tenancy become payable under the demoted tenancy
  - It is also a term of the demoted tenancy that any rent paid in advance or overpaid at the termination of the secure tenancy is credited to the tenant's liability to pay rent under the demoted tenancy [s.82A(2); (3) HA 1985]

- The court must not make a Demotion Order unless it is satisfied that:

- The tenant or person residing in or visiting the dwelling-house has engaged or threatened to engage in conduct to which s.s.153A or 153B Housing Act 1996 (anti-social behaviour or use of premises for unlawful purposes) applies, and
- It is reasonable to make the order [s.82A(4) HA 1985]

■ S.14(4) ASBA 2003 also introduces into the Housing Act 1988 a s.6A **(demotion because of anti-social behaviour)** which applies to an **assured** tenancy if the landlord is a registered social landlord [6A(1) HA 1988]

■ The landlord may apply to a county court for a Demotion Order which has the following effect:

- The assured tenancy is terminated with effect from the date specified in the order
- If the tenant remains in occupation of the dwelling house after that date a demoted tenancy is created with effect from that date
- It is a term of the demoted tenancy that any arrears of rent payable at the termination of the assured tenancy become payable under the demoted tenancy
- It is also a term of the demoted tenancy that any rent paid in advance or overpaid at the termination of the assured tenancy is credited to the tenant's liability to pay rent under the demoted tenancy [s.6A(2); (3) HA 1988]

- The court must not make a Demotion Order unless it is satisfied that:

  - The tenant or person residing in or visiting the dwelling-house has engaged or threatened to engage in conduct to which s.s.153A or 153B Housing Act 1996 (anti-social behaviour or use of premises for unlawful purposes) applies, and
  - It is reasonable to make the order [s.6A(4) HA 1988]

- The court must not entertain proceedings for a Demotion Order unless:

  - The landlord has served notice on the tenant under sub-section (6) or
  - The court thinks it is just and equitable to dispense with the requirement of the notice [s.6A(5) HA 1998]

- The notice must:

  - Give particulars of the conduct in respect of which the order is being sought
  - State that the proceedings will not begin before the date specified in the notice
  - State that the proceedings will not begin after the end of the 12 month period beginning with the date of service of notice [s.6A(6) HA 1998]

NB. The date specified for the purpose of the second bullet point in sub-section (6) above must not be before 2 weeks beginning with the date of service of the notice [s.6A(7) HA 1998]

- S.15 ASBA 2003 inserts a new s.20B into the Housing Act 1998 (**demoted assured shorthold tenancies**) and confirms that it applies if:

  - The tenancy is created by virtue of an order of the court under s.82A HA 1985 or s.6A of HA 1998 and
  - The landlord is a registered social landlord

- At the end of 1 year starting with the day when the Demotion Order takes effect, a demoted assured shorthold tenancy ceases to be an assured shorthold tenancy unless sub-section (3) applies (i.e. if before the 1 year, the landlord gives notice of proceedings for possession) [s.20B(2); (3) HA 1998]

- If sub-section (3) applies, the tenancy continues to be a demoted assured shorthold tenancy until the end of the year cited in sub-section (2), or (if later) until either:

  - Notice of proceedings for possession is withdrawn
  - Proceedings are determined in favour of the tenant
  - The period of 6 months from the date notice is given, ends and no proceedings for possession have been brought [s.20B(4) HA 1998]

Proceedings for Possession: Anti-social Behaviour [s. 16 ASBA 2003]

■ S.16(1) ASBA 2003 introduces a new s.85A into the Housing Act 1985 and a new s.9A into the Housing Act 1988 (**proceedings for possession: anti-social behaviour**) and requires the court, in considering whether it is reasonable to make a Possession Order on the grounds of the conduct of the tenant or other person) to consider in particular:

- The effect that the nuisance or annoyance has had on persons other than the person against whom the order is sought
- Any continuing effect the nuisance or annoyance is likely to have on such persons
- The effect that the nuisance or annoyance would be likely to have on such persons if the conduct is repeated

Part 3: Parental Responsibilities

Parenting Orders [s.8 Crime & Disorder Act 1998 as amended by s.18 ASBA 2003]

■ A court must not make a Parenting Order unless it has been notified by the Secretary of State that arrangements for implementing them are available in the area where it appears to the court the parent resides/will reside and the notice had not been withdrawn [s.8 (3) CDA 1998]. A Home Office letter of 27.04.00 confirmed arrangements were in place in all areas from 01.06.00.

Conditions [s.8 (1); (6) CDA 1998]

■ The court **may** impose a Parenting Order if, in any court proceedings (as well as satisfying the 'relevant condition' described in the following paragraph):

  • A Child Safety Order is made in respect of a child
  • An Anti-social Behaviour Order or Sex Offender Order is made with respect to a child/young person

NB. S.2 CDA 1998 (Sex Offender Orders) was actually repealed by SOA 2003 Sch.7 and although the Home Office intended to insert the new 'Sexual Offences Prevention Order, it overlooked the need to introduce the necessary amendment to the SOA 2003.

- A child/young person is convicted of an offence or
- A person is convicted of an offence under s.443 (failure to comply with School Attendance Order) or s.444 (failure to secure regular attendance at school of registered pupil) Education Act 1996

- ■ The relevant condition that must be satisfied is that the Parenting Order would be desirable in the interests of preventing:

  - (Where relevant) any repetition of the kind of behaviour which led to the Child Safety, Anti-social or Sex Offender Order (see italicised foot note above) being made
  - (Where relevant) the commission of any further offence by the child/young person
  - (Where relevant) the commission of any further offence under s.443 or s.444 Education Act 1996

Effect of Parenting Order made under CDA 1998

- ■ A Parenting Order requires the parent:

  - To comply, for a period of not more than 12 months with such requirements as are specified in the order and
  - To attend for a concurrent period not exceeding 3 months such counselling or guidance sessions as may be specified in directions given by the responsible officer [s.8(4) CDA 1998 as substituted by s.18 ASBA 2003]

NB. If a Parenting Order has previously been made in respect of the parent, it may, but need not, include the requirements for counselling/guidance as described above [s.8 (5) CDA 1998].

■ Requirements that may be specified in the order are those the court considers desirable in the interests of preventing any such repetition, or as the case may be, the commission of any such further offence [s.8 (7)].

■ A counselling or guidance programme which a parent is required to attend by virtue of subsection (4)(b) may be, or include a residential course **if** the court is satisfied that:

• The attendance of the parent is likely to more effective than her/his attendance at a non-residential course in preventing any such repetition or as the case may be, the commission of any such further offence and

• Any interference with family life which is likely to result from the attendance is proportionate [s.8(7A) CDA 1998 inserted by s.18 ASBA 2003]

■ If an Anti-social Behaviour Order is made in respect of an under 16 year old, the court:

• Must make a Parenting Order if satisfied that he relevant condition is satisfied

• If it is not satisfied, must state in open court that it is not and why [s.9(1B) CDA 1998 inserted by s.85 ASBA 2003]

*NB. The responsible officer for purposes of a
Parenting Order is a probation officer, social worker
of a local authority social services or YOT member
(one of whom will be specified) [s.8(8) CDA 1998].*

Procedural Requirements [Sch.34 CJA 2003]

■ Where a person **under the age of 16** is convicted
of an offence, the court which convicts her/him,
unless prohibited from so doing because it has
made a Referral Order **must**:

- If it is satisfied that the relevant condition is
fulfilled, make a Parenting Order and
- If not satisfied, state this and reasons in open
court [s.9(1A) and (2A)–(2B) inserted by CJA
2003 Sch.34 para.2]

*NB. Court has discretion to consider making a
Parenting Order in case of 16 or 17 year olds.*

■ In the following situations, before making a
Parenting Order a court must obtain and consider
information about the person's family
circumstances and likely effect of the order on
those circumstances:

- A Child Safety Order is made
- An under 16 year old convicted of an offence
or made the subject of An Anti-social Behaviour
Order or Sexual Offences Order (see italicised
footnote on page. 26) or
- Is convicted of failure to comply with a School
Attendance Order or to secure regular

attendance at school where the person concerned is under 16. [s.9 (2) CDA 1998].

■ Where a court proposes to make both a Referral Order and a Parenting Order it must first obtain and consider a report from an appropriate officer:

• Indicating the requirements proposed by that officer to be included in the Parenting Order
• Indicating the reasons why s/he considers those requirements desirable to prevent further offences
• (In the case of an under 16 year old) containing information about her/his family circumstances and the likely effect of the order on those [s.9(2A) CDA 1998 inserted by Sch.34 CJA 2003]

■ Before making a Parenting Order, a court must explain to the parent in ordinary language, the:

• Effect of the order and of the requirements proposed to be included within it
• Consequences which may follow under sub-section (7) (see below) if s/he fails to comply with any of those requirements and that
• Court has power (sub-section (5)) to review the order on the application either of the parent or of the responsible officer [s.9(3) CDA 1998]

NB. Requirements specified in, and directions given in a Parenting Order must, as far as practicable, avoid any conflict with a parent's religious beliefs and any interference with times, if any, at which s/he

*normally works or attends an educational
establishment [s.9 (4) CDA 1998].*

Variation and Discharge

■ If, while a Parenting Order is in force it appears
to the court which made it, on the application of
responsible officer or parent, that it is appropriate
to do so, the court can vary or discharge the
order by:

- Cancelling any provision included in it or
- Inserting in it (in addition to or instead of any
  existing provision) any provision that could have
  been included in the order if the court had then
  had power to make it and were exercising that
  power [s.9 (5) CDA 1998].

*NB. Where an application to discharge is dismissed,
no further application for its discharge can be made
by any person except with the consent of the court
which made the order [s.9 (6) CDA 1998].*

Failure to Comply with Requirements
[s.9 (7) CDA 1998]

■ If, while a Parenting Order is in force, the parent
without reasonable excuse fails to comply with
any requirement included in the order or specified
in directions given by the responsible officer,
s/he is liable on summary conviction to a fine
not exceeding level 3 on the standard scale.

Appeals [s.10 CDA 1998]

■ With respect to Parenting Orders made by virtue of Child Safety Orders, appeals are to the High Court [s.10(1)(a) CDA 1998].

■ With respect to Parenting Orders made by virtue of an Anti-social Behaviour Orders, appeals are to the Crown Court [s.10 (1) (b) CDA 1998].

■ In either case the court may:

• Make such orders as may be necessary to give effect to its determination of the appeal and
• Also make such incidental or consequential orders as appears to it to be just [s.10(2) CDA 1998]

NB. Any order made by the High Court or Crown Court in response to an appeal (other than one directing an application be re-heard by a magistrates' court) is to be treated as if it were an order of the court from which appeal was brought, not an order of the High Court or Crown Court [s.10(3) CDA 1998].

■ A person in respect of whom a Parenting Order is made for failure to secure regular school attendance has the same right of appeal as if the order were a sentence passed on her/him for the offence which led to the order [s.10 (5) CDA 1998].

■ A person in respect of whom a Parenting Order is made where a child/young person is convicted of an offence has the same right to appeal as if the offence were an offence committed by her/him and the order were a sentence passed on her/him for the offence [s.10 (4) CDA 1998].

NB. The Lord Chancellor is empowered to make provision in appeals relating to Parenting Orders, made by virtue of Child Safety Orders, about transfer of cases to alternative courts [s.10 (6) CDA 1998].

Parenting Contracts in Cases of Exclusion from School or Truancy [s.19 ASBA 2003]

■ Where a pupil has been excluded on disciplinary grounds from a relevant school for a fixed period or permanently, or where a child of compulsory school age has failed to attend regularly at a relevant school at which s/he is a registered pupil:

   • A local education authority (LEA) or the governing body of a relevant school may enter into a Parenting Contract with a parent of the pupil or child [s.19 (1)–(3) ASBA 2003]

■ A **Parenting Contract** is a document (which must be signed by a parent and on behalf of LEA or governing body) which contains:

   • A statement by the parent that s/he agrees to comply with such requirements (which may include in particular a requirement to attend a counselling or guidance programme) as may be specified in the document for such period as may be so specified, and
   • A statement by the LEA or governing body that it agrees to provide support to the parent for the purpose of complying with those requirements [s.19(4);(5);(7) ASBA 2003]

■ The purpose of the requirements is (as the case may be) to:

- Improve the behaviour of the pupil or
- Ensure that the child attends regularly at the relevant school at which s/he is registered [s.19(6) ASBA 2003]

Parenting Orders in Cases of Exclusion from School [s.20 ASBA 2003]

■ Where a pupil has been excluded on disciplinary grounds from a relevant school for a fixed period or permanently and such conditions as may be prescribed in regulations made by (in England) the Secretary of State, and in Wales the Welsh Assembly are satisfied:

- A local education authority (LEA) may apply to the magistrates' court for a Parenting Order in respect of a parent of a pupil [s.20(1); (2) ASBA 2003]

■ If such an application is made, the court may make a Parenting Order in respect of a parent of the pupil if satisfied that making the order would be desirable in the interests of improving the behaviour of the pupil [s.20(3) ASBA 2003]

■ A Parenting Order is an order which requires the parent:

- To comply, for a period not exceeding 12 months, with such requirements as are specified in the order and
- Subject to sub-section (5) outlined below, to attend for a concurrent period not exceeding 3 months, such counselling or guidance programme as may be specified in directions

given by the responsible officer [s.20(4) ASBA 2003]

NB. In any case where a Parenting Order has previously been made in respect of a parent under s.20 or any other enactment it may, but need not, include a requirement to attend counselling/guidance[s.20(5) ASBA 2003].

■ A counselling or guidance programme which a parent is obliged to attend by virtue of s.20(4)(b) ASBA 2003 may be or include a residential course but only if the court is satisfied that the following 2 conditions are satisfied:

   • The parent's attendance at a residential course is likely to be more effective than her/his attendance at a non-residential course in improving the behaviour of the pupil
   • That any interference with family life which is likely to result from the attendance of the parent at a residential course is proportionate in all the circumstances [s.20(6)–(8) ASBA 2003]

■ In deciding whether to make a Parenting Order under s.20, a court must take into account (amongst other things):

   • Any refusal by the parent to enter into a Parenting Contract under s.19 in respect of a pupil falling within s.19(1) or
   • If the parent has entered into such a Parenting Contract, any failure by the parent to comply

with the requirements specified in the contract [s.21(1) ASBA 2003]

NB. Before making a Parenting Order under s.20 in the case of an under 16 year old, a court must obtain and consider information about the pupil's family circumstance and the likely effect of the order on those circumstances [s.21(2) ASBA 2003]

■ LEAs, head teachers and responsible officers must, in carrying out their functions in relation to Parenting Orders, have regard to any guidance which is issued from time to time, by (in England) the Secretary of State, and in Wales the Welsh Assembly [s.21(5) ASBA 2003]

NB. The Secretary of State/Welsh Assembly may by regulations make provision as to how costs associated with the requirements of Parenting Orders under s.20 (including costs of providing counselling or guidance) are to be borne [s.21(4) ASBA 2003]

Parenting Order: Appeals [s.22]

■ The Crown Court will hear appeals against the making of a Parenting Order made under s.20 [s.22 (1) ASBA 2003].

■ The court may:

- Make such orders as may be necessary to give effect to its determination of the appeal and
- Also make such incidental or consequential orders as appears to it to be just [s.22(2) ASBA 2003]

NB. Any order made by the Crown Court in response to an appeal (other than one directing an application be re-heard by a magistrates' court) is to be treated as if it were an order of the court from which appeal was brought, not an order of the Crown Court [s.10(3) CDA 1998].

Penalty Notices for Parents in Cases of Truancy [s.444A EA 1996 inserted by 23 ASBA 2003]

■ An authorised officer may give the person a Penalty Notice in respect of that offence where s/he has reason to believe that:

- The person has committed an offence under s.444 (1) EA 1996 (parental failure to ensure school aged child attends school at which s/he is registered)
- The school to which the offence relates is a relevant school in England [s.444A(1) EA 1996]

■ A Penalty Notice is a notice offering a person the opportunity of discharging any liability to conviction for the s.444 (1) offence by paying a penalty [s.444A (2) EA 1996], and proceedings for an offence may not be instituted before the end of such period as may be prescribed [s.444A (3) EA 1996].

NB. A person given a Penalty Notice cannot be convicted of the offence to which the notice relates if s/he pays the penalty (which is payable to local education authorities in England) [s.444A (4); (5) EA 1996].

■ Regulations may specify further details of Penalty Notices e.g. amount of penalty, time to pay, method of payment, who may be authorised to give notices etc [s.444B(1) EA 1996].

NB. For the purposes of Penalty Notices for parents in case of truancy, an 'authorised officer' may be a constable (or community support officer), an authorised local education officer (likely to be education welfare officers) , a head teacher or authorised teacher and a 'relevant school' means a maintained school, a pupil referrals unit, an academy, city technical college or a city college for the technology of the arts [s.444B(4) EA 1996]

Parenting Contracts in Respect of Criminal Conduct and Anti-social Behaviour [s.25 ASBA 2003]

■ Where a child or young person has been referred to a youth offending team (YOT), the team may enter into a Parenting Contract with the parent of the child/young person if a member of the team has reason to believe that the child/young person has engaged, or is likely to engage in criminal conduct or anti-social behaviour [s.25 (1); (2) ASBA 2003].

■ A Parenting Contract is a document (which must be signed by the parent and on behalf of the YOT) which contains:

- A statement by the parent that s/he agrees to comply with such requirements as may be specified in the document for such period as may be so specified
- A statement by the YOT that it agrees to provide support to the parent for the purpose of complying with those requirements [s.25(3); (6) ASBA 2003]

■ The requirements referred to above may include in particular a requirement to attend a counselling to guidance programme and the purpose of the requirements is to prevent the child/young person from engaging in, or further engaging in criminal conduct or anti-social behaviour [s.25(4); (5) ASBA 2003].

NB. Parenting Orders have previously been available only for those actually convicted of a criminal offence. This new provision allows the possibility of earlier intervention.

Parenting Orders in Respect of Criminal Conduct and Anti-social Behaviour [s.26 ASBA 2003]

■ Where a child or young person has been referred to a YOT, a member of that team may apply to a magistrates' court for a Parenting Order in respect of a parent of that child/young person [s.26(1);(2) ASBA 2003].

■ If such an application is made, the court may make a Parenting Order in respect of a parent of the child/young person if it is satisfied that:

- The child/young person has engaged in criminal conduct or anti-social behaviour and that
- Making the order would be desirable in the interests of preventing the child/young person from engaging in further criminal conduct or further anti-social behaviour [s.26(3) ASBA 2003]

■ A Parenting Order requires the parent:

- To comply, for a period of not more than 12 months with such requirements as are specified in the order and
- To attend for a concurrent period not exceeding 3 months such counselling or guidance sessions as may be specified in directions given by the responsible officer [s.26(4) ASBA 2003]

NB. If a Parenting Order has previously been made in respect of the parent, it may, but need not, include the requirements for counselling/guidance as described above [s.26 (5) ASBA 2003].

■ A counselling or guidance programme which a parent is required to attend by virtue of subsection (4)(b) may be, or include a residential course **if** the court is satisfied that:

  • The attendance of the parent is likely to more effective than her/his attendance at a non-residential course in preventing the child or young person from engaging in further criminal conduct or further any-social behaviour
  • Any interference with family life which is likely to result from the attendance is proportionate [s.26 (6)–(8) ASBA 2003]

■ In deciding whether to make a Parenting Order under s.26 a court must take into account (amongst other things):

  • Any refusal by the parent to enter into a Parenting Contract under s.25 in respect of the child or young person, or
  • If the parent has entered into such a Parenting Contract, any failure by the parent to comply with the requirements specified in the contract [s.27(1) ASBA 2003]

■ Before making a Parenting Order under s.26 in the case of a child/young person aged less than 16, a court must obtain and consider information about her/his family's circumstances and the likely effect of the order on those circumstances [s.26(2) ASBA 2003].

■ Before making a Parenting Order, a court must explain to the parent in ordinary language:

- The effect of the order and of the requirements proposed to be included within it
- The consequences which may follow under sub-section (7) (see below) if s/he fails to comply with any of those requirements and that
- The court has power (sub-section (5)) to review the order on the application either of the parent or of the responsible officer [s.9(3) CDA 1998]

NB. Requirements specified in, and directions given in a Parenting Order must, as far as practicable, avoid any conflict with a parent's religious beliefs and any interference with times, if any, at which s/he normally works or attends an educational establishment [s.9 (4) CDA 1998].

■ If, while a Parenting Order is in force it appears to the court which made it, on the application of responsible officer or parent, that it is appropriate to do so, the court can vary or discharge the order by:

- Cancelling any provision included in it or
- Inserting in it (in addition to or instead of any existing provision) any provision that could have been included in the order if the court had then had power to make it and were exercising that power [s.9 (5) CDA 1998].

NB. Where an application to discharge is dismissed, no further application for its discharge can be made by any person except with the consent of the court which made the order [s.9 (6) CDA 1998].

■ If, while a Parenting Order is in force, the parent without reasonable excuse fails to comply with any requirement included in the order or specified in directions given by the responsible officer, s/he is liable on summary conviction to a fine not exceeding level 3 on the standard scale [s.9 (7) CDA 1998].

Appeals Against Parenting Orders [s.28 ASBA 2003]

■ An appeal against a Parenting Order made under s.26 lies to the Crown Court [s.28 (1) ASBA 2003].

NB. 'Anti-social behaviour' in sections 25–28 ASBA 2003 means behaviour by a person which causes or is likely to cause harassment, alarm or distress to one or more other persons not of the same household as the person and 'criminal conduct' means conduct which constitutes a criminal offence or in the case of conduct by an under 10 year old, would constitute a criminal offence if s/he were 10 or over [s.29 (1) ASBA 2003].

Part 4: Dispersal of Groups etc

Dispersal of Groups and Removal of Persons Under 16 to Their Place of Residence [s.30 ASBA 2003]

- The relevant officer may give an authorisation that the powers conferred on a constable in uniform by sub-sections (3)–(6) ASBA 2003 (described below) are to be exercisable for a period specified in the authorisation, not exceeding 6 months, if the relevant officer has reasonable grounds for believing that:

  - Any members of the public have been intimidated, harassed, alarmed or distressed as a result of the presence or behaviour of groups or 2 or more persons in public places in any locality in her/his police area (the 'relevant locality')
  - Anti-social behaviour is a significant and persistent problem in the relevant locality [s.30(1) ASBA 2003]

  NB. A British Transport Police Force officer may provide s.30 authorisation for the area which forms part of property in relation to which s/he has all the powers and privileges of a constable by virtue of s.31(1)(a) to (f) Railways and Transport Safety Act 2003 [s.35(1) ASBA 2003].

- If a constable in uniform has reasonable grounds for believing that the presence of or behaviour of a group of 2 or more persons in any public place in the relevant locality has resulted, or is likely to result, in any members of the public being intimidated, harassed, alarmed or distressed, s/he may give 1 or more of the following:

- A direction requiring the persons in the group to disperse (either immediately or by such time and in such a way as s/he may specify)
- A direction requiring any of those persons whose place of residence is not within the relevant locality to leave that locality or any part of it (either immediately or by such time and in such a way as s/he may specify)
- A direction prohibiting any of those persons whose place of residence is not within the relevant locality from returning to it or any part of it for such a period (not exceeding 24 hours) from the giving of the direction as s/he may specify [s.30(4) ASBA 2003]

■ A direction under s.30(4) may be:

- Given orally
- Given to any person individually or to 2 or more persons together and
- Withdrawn or varied by the person who gave it [s.32(1) ASBA 2003]

■ A person who knowingly contravenes a direction given to her/him under s.30(4) commits an offence and is liable on summary conviction to:

- A fine not exceeding level 4 on the standard scale

- Imprisonment for term not exceeding 3 months or both [s.32(2) ASBA 2003]

NB. A constable in uniform may arrest without warrant any person s/he reasonably suspects has committed an offence under s.32 (2).

s.30 (4) directions cannot be given to those engaged in lawful Trades Union activity or lawfully arranged public processions [s.30 (5) (a) ASBA 2003].

■ A constable in uniform may, between 9pm and 6am, remove a person to her/his place of residence (unless the constable has reasonable grounds for believing the person would thus suffer significant harm) **if** s/he finds that person in any public place in the relevant locality and has reasonable grounds for believing that the person is:

- Under the age of 16 and
- Not under the effective control of a parent or a responsible person aged 18 or over [s.30(6) ASBA 2003]

Obtaining & Withdrawing Authorisation [ss.31–32 ASBA 2003]

■ The authorisation required under s.30 must:

- Be in writing
- Be signed by the relevant officer giving it
- Specify the relevant locality, grounds on which authorisation given and the period for which the powers conferred by s.30(3)–(6) are exercisable [s.31(1) ASBA 2003]

■ An authorisation may not be given without the consent of the local authority or each local authority whose are includes the whole of part of the relevant locality [s.31 (2) ASBA 2003].

■ Publicity must be given to an authorisation by either or both of the following methods:

- Publishing an authorisation notice in a newspaper circulating in the relevant locality
- Posting an authorisation notice in some conspicuous place or places within the relevant locality [s.31(3) ASBA 2003]

NB. The requirements to publicise must be satisfied before the powers conferred by sub-section 3–6 are exercisable [s.31(5) ASBA 2003]

■ An authorisation may be withdrawn by:

- The relevant officer who gave it or
- Any other relevant officer whose police area includes the relevant locality and whose rank is the same as or higher than that of the relevant officer who gave it [s.31(6)(a) ASBA 2003]

■ Before the withdrawal of authorisation, consultation must take place with any local authority whose area includes the whole or part of the relevant locality [s.31(7) ASBA 2003]

Powers of Community Support Officers [s.33 ASBA 2003]

- S.33 amends the Police Reform Act 2002 to allow community support officers to be given the powers to disperse groups and remove persons under 16 to their place of residence as described in s. 30 above (community support officers are civilian employees of police forces designated by chief officers to exercise a range of powers within the relevant police area).

Code of Practice [s.34 ASBA 2003]

- The Secretary of State may issue from time to time a code of practice about the use of s.30 powers and relevant officers and those exercising the s.30(3)–(6) powers must have regard to the current version.

Part 5: Firearms

Possession of Air Weapon or Imitation Firearm in a Public Place [s.37 ASBA 2003]

■ This section amends s.19 FA 1968, which deals with the carrying of firearms in a public place, so as to include air weapons and imitation firearms.

■ S.37(1) ASBA 2003 amends s.19 FA 1968 (offence to carry firearm in public place) so that the list of prohibited weapons becomes:

- A loaded shot gun
- An air weapon (loaded or not)
- Any other firearm (loaded or not) together with ammunition suitable for use in that firearm, or
- An imitation firearm

■ An 'imitation firearm' is defined in s. 57(4) FA 1968 and covers anything which has the appearance of being a firearm whether or not it is capable of discharging a shot or bullet.

NB. S.37 (3) ASBA 2003 makes this an arrestable offence by adding the new offence to the list of arrestable offences set out in Schedule 1A to the Police and Criminal Evidence Act 1984. This will be subject to a maximum penalty of 6 months imprisonment.

Air Weapons: Age Limits
[s.38 ASBA 2003]

■ s.38 amends ss. 22, 23 and 24 FA 1968 to change the age at which a young person may own an air weapon and restrict when it may be used unsupervised.

■ The present limit for acquisition and possession is raised from 14 to 17 and it is an offence for anybody to give an air weapon to a person under seventeen [s.22(4) FA 1968 as amended by s.38(2) ASBA 2003]

NB. This means no-one under 17 is able to have an air weapon in her/his possession at any time unless supervised by someone aged at least 21 or as part of an approved target shooting club or gallery.

■ 14 to 16 year olds inclusive will be permitted to have air weapons unsupervised when on private land, provided they have the consent of the occupier. It will be an offence for them to shoot beyond the boundaries of that land [s.23(4) FA 1968 as amended by ASBA 2003]

NB. See also CAE's companion guide 'How Old Do I Have to Be To ...? for comprehensive information about rights and responsibilities at various ages.

Prohibition of Certain Air Weapons [s.39 ASBA 2003]

- S.39 contains a ban on air weapons that use the self-contained gas cartridge system, which are vulnerable to conversion to fire conventional ammunition.

- S.39 also adds the weapons to section 5(1) FA1968, thereby making them prohibited weapons which cannot be possessed, purchased, acquired, manufactured, sold or transferred without the authority of the Secretary of State (provision is made for existing owners of the weapons to retain possession, provided they obtained a firearms certificate from the police before 30.04.04).

NB. S.39(6) ASBA 2003 also creates an order making power that will enable the Secretary of State to prohibit or introduce other controls in respect of any air weapon which appears to her/him to be especially dangerous.

Part 6: The Environment

Closure of Noisy Premises [s.40 ASBA 2003]

- The chief executive officer of the relevant local authority may make a 'Closure Notice' in relation to premises to which s.40 applies (e.g. pubs and night clubs) if s/he reasonably believes that:

  - A public nuisance is being caused by noise coming from the premises and
  - The closure of the premises is necessary to prevent that nuisance [s.40(1);(2) ASBA 2003]

- A Closure Order is one which requires specified premises to be kept closed during a specified period:

  - Not exceeding 24 hours and
  - Beginning when a manager of premises receives written notice of the order [s.40(3) ASBA 2003]

- A person commits an offence if without reasonable cause, s/he permits premises to be open in contravention of a Closure Order [s.40 (4) ASBA 2003].

- A person guilty of an offence under s.40 is liable on summary conviction to:

  - Imprisonment for term not exceeding 3 months
  - A fine not exceeding £20,000 or
  - Both [s.40(5) ASBA 2003]

Dealing with Noise at Night [s.42 ASBA 2003]

■ S.42 extends the power of environmental health officers to issue a warning for noise in a domestic dwelling at night and, if it continues issue a fixed penalty notice of £100.

■ Every local authority in England and Wales may now, in response to a complaint about such noise arrange for an officer of that authority to take reasonable steps to investigate the complaint.

NB. The local authority may now retain the proceeds of its penalty receipts for the purposes of further application of the ASBA 2003 or other actions which may be specified by the Secretary of State [s.1(5) Noise Act 1996 as substituted by s.42(1) ASBA 2003].

Penalty Notices for Graffiti and Fly-Posting

■ Where an authorised officer of a local authority has reason to believe that a person has committed a 'relevant' offence in the area of that authority, s/he may give that person a notice offering her/him the opportunity of discharging any liability to conviction for that offence by payment of a penalty in accordance with the notice [s.43 (1) ASBA 2003].

NB. Unless the Secretary of State (England) or Welsh Assembly (Wales) substitute a different amount, the penalty payable under s.43 (1) is £50 [s.43 (10); (11) ASBA 2003].

■ A 'relevant' offence is defined in s.44(1) ASBA 2003 as an offence under:

- Paragraph 10 of s.54 Metropolitan Police Act 1839 (affixing posters etc)
- S.20(1) London County Council (General Powers) Act 1954 (defacement of streets with slogans etc)
- S.1(1) Criminal Damage Act 1971 (damaging property etc) which involves only the painting or writing on, or soiling, marking or other defacing of any property by whatever means
- S.131(2) Highways Act 1980 (including that provision as applied by s.27(6) Countryside Act 1968 which involves only an act of obliteration

- S.132(1) Highways Act 1980 (painting or affixing things on structures on the highway etc)
- S.224(3) Town and Country Planning Act 1990 (displaying advertisement in contravention of regulations)

■ An authorised officer may **not** give such a notice if s/he considers that the commission of the offence:

- In the case of one falling within s.44(1)(c) i.e. s1(1) CDA 1971 (damaging property etc) which involves only the painting or writing on, or soiling, marking or other defacing of any property by whatever means **also** involves an offence under s.30 CDA 1998 i.e. is racially aggravated
- In the case of any other relevant offence, was motivated (wholly or partly) by hostility either toward a person based upon membership or presumed membership of a racial or religious group or towards members of a racial or religious group based on their membership of that group [s.43(2) ASBA 2003]

■ In the case of a relevant offence falling within s.44(1)(f) i.e. an offence under s.224(3) Town and Country Planning Act 1990 (displaying advertisement in contravention of regulations), an authorised officer may **not** give a notice to a person under s.43(1) in relation to the display of an advertisement unless s/he has reason to believe that that person personally affixed or placed the advertisement to, against or upon the land or object on which the advertisement is or was displayed [s.43(3) ASBA 2003].

■ Where a person is given notice as per. s.43(1) in respect of an offence:

- No proceedings may be instituted for that offence (or any other relevant offence arising out of the same circumstances) before 14 days after the date of the notice
- S/he may not be convicted of that offence (or any other relevant offence arising out of the same circumstances) if, before those 14 days have elapsed, s/he pays the penalty [s.43 (4) ASBA 2003]

■ A notice under s.43(1) must give such particulars of the circumstances alleged to constitute the offence as are necessary for giving reasonable information of the offence and must state the:

- Period during which, proceedings will not be instituted for the offence
- Amount of the penalty
- Person to whom and the address at which the penalty may be paid [s.43(5),(6) ASBA 2003]

NB. Penalties payable under s.43 (1) are to the local authority which may retain the penalty receipts and apply them for further comparable responses or as required by regulation [s.45 ASBA 2003].

Powers of Police Civilians [s.46 ASBA 2003]

■ s.46(1) ASBA 2003 amends Schedule 4 PRA 2002 to include powers for a community support officer to issue penalty notices in respect of graffiti and fly posting (as they currently have for issuing penalties in respect of littering and dog fouling).

■ S.46(2) amends Schedule 5 PRA 2002 in respect of powers of accredited persons to issue fixed penalty notices to include 'authorised officers of the local authority' being able to do so in respect of graffiti and fly-posting.

NB. An authorised officer means an officer of the local authority who is authorised in writing by the authority for the purpose of giving notices under s.43(1) ASBA 2003 [s.47(1) ASBA 2003].

Graffiti Removal Notices
[s.48 ASBA 2003]

- The local authority may serve a 'Graffiti Removal Notice' upon any person who is responsible for that surface e.g. railways or port authorities imposing requirements specified in s.48(3) (see below) where it is satisfied that:

  - A relevant surface in an area has been defaced by graffiti and that
  - The defacement is detrimental to the amenity of the area or is offensive [s.48(1); (2) ASBA 2003]

- The requirement enabled by s.48(3) is that the defacement be removed, cleared or otherwise remedied within a period specified in the notice being not less than 28 days beginning with the day the notice is served [s.48(3) ASBA 2003].

- If the above requirement is not complied with, the local authority or any person authorised by it may remove, clear or otherwise remedy the defacement and the authority or the person authorised by it may enter any land to the extent reasonably necessary for that purpose [s.48 (4),(5) ASBA 2003].

  NB. A Graffiti Removal Notice must explain the effect of s.48(4);(5) and ss.49 and 51 [s.48(6) ASBA 2003]

- Where after reasonable enquiry, a local authority is unable to ascertain the name or proper address of any person who is responsible for a relevant surface, it may affix a Graffiti Removal Notice to the surface, enter any land to the extent reasonably necessary for that purpose and that notice will be regarded as having been served upon a person responsible for surface [s.48(8) ASBA 2003]

NB. A local authority may recover from the person on whom a Graffiti Removal Notice was served (and subject to having served on that person notice setting out the amount and details of the expenditure it proposes to recover) expenditure reasonably incurred in exercise of its power under s.48(4) ASBA 2003 [s.49 ASBA 2003].

Appeals [s.51 ASBA 2003]

- A person on whom a Graffiti Removal Notice is served may, within 21 days of its service, appeal against the notice to a magistrates' court on the grounds that:

  - The defacement is neither detrimental to the amenity of the area nor offensive
  - There is a material defect or error in, or connection with, the notice
  - The notice should have been served on another person [s.51(1), (2) ASBA 2003]

- Where an appeal under s.51 (1) is brought, the Graffiti Removal Notice is of no effect pending the final determination or withdrawal of the appeal [s.51 (3) ASBA 2003].

- On determination of such an appeal, the magistrates' court must either:

  - Quash the notice
  - Modify the notice
  - Dismiss the appeal [s.51(4) ASBA 2003]

- Where the court modifies the notice or dismisses the appeal, it may extend the period specified in the notice [s.51 (5) ASBA 2003].

- A person on whom a notice under s.49(2) is served may, within 21 days of the day on which it is served, appeal to a magistrates' court on the grounds that the expenditure which the authority is proposing to recover is excessive [s.51(6) ASBA 2003].

- On the determination of an appeal under s.51(6) ASBA 2003, the magistrates' court must either:

  - Confirm that the amount which the authority is proposing to recover is reasonable or
  - Substitute a lower amount which the authority is entitled to recover [s.51(7) ASBA 2003]

NB. S.52 ASBA 2003 provides some qualified protection for the authority or those acting on its behalf in exercising s.48 powers to enter premises and/or removing graffiti etc.

Display of Advertisements in Contravention of Regulations [s.53 ASBA 2003]

- S.53 changes the penalty for the offence of displaying advertisements in contravention of regulations under the Town and Country Planning Act 1990 from being subject to a level 3 fine (maximum £1,000) to level 4 (maximum £2,500).

Sale of Aerosol Paint to Children [s.54 ASBA 2003]

■ A person commits an offence if s/he sells an aerosol paint container to a person under the age of 16 [s.54 (1) ASBA 2003].

NB. An aerosol paint container is a device which contains paint stored under pressure and is designed to permit the release of the paint as a spray [s.54 (2) ASBA 2003].

■ A person guilty of an offence under s.54 is liable on summary conviction to a fine not exceeding level 4 on the standard scale [s.54 (3) ASBA 2003].

■ It is a defence for a person charged with an offence under s.54 in respect of a sale to prove that s/he:

- Took all reasonable steps to determine the purchaser's age and
- Reasonably believed that the purchaser was not under 16 [s.54(4) ASBA 2003]

■ It is a defence for a person charged with an offence under s.54 in respect of a sale effected by another person to prove that s/he (the defendant) took all reasonable steps to avoid the commission of an offence under s.54 [s.54(5) ASBA 2003].

Unlawfully Deposited Waste etc [s.55 ASBA 2003]

- S.55 amends the Control of Pollution (Amendment) Act 1989 and the Environmental Protection Act 1990 to have the following effect.

- Local authorities will have additional powers to investigate and tackle fly-tipping which have only been available to the Environment Agency e.g. the power to stop, search and seize a vehicle being used to fly-tip waste and the power to investigate incidents in order to track down and prosecute those responsible for dumping the waste.

Extension of Litter Authority Powers to Take Remedial Action [s.56 ASBA 2003]

- Local authorities can already issue a Litter Abatement Notice requiring the owner of the land to clean it and if this is ignored, can enter the land, clear it of litter and recover the cost through the courts.

- S.56 removes an exemption that prevents local authorities from entering and clearing Crown land or the land of statutory undertakers e.g. railways and port authorities (though Crown land occupied for armed forces purposes remains exempt).

Part 7: Public Order & Trespass

Public Assemblies [s.57 ASBA 2003]

■ New powers relating to public assemblies are introduced by s.57 ASBA 2003. s.16 Public Order Act 1986 which defines 'public assembly' for the purposes of the powers in s.14 of that Act, is amended so that directions imposing conditions may be issued to as few as 2 (rather than what was 20) people.

NB. The senior police officer must though reasonably believe that the public assembly may result in serious public disorder, serious disruption to the life of the community, or the purpose of the persons organising the assembly is the intimidation of others with a view to compelling them not to do something they have a right to do, or to do something that they have a right not to do.

Raves [s.58 ASBA 2003]

■ S.63 Criminal Justice and Public Order Act 1994
(CJPOA 1994) is amended to allow the police to
direct participants at indoor raves to leave buildings
where trespass is involved and to include events
of 20 people or more (previous law specified 100
or more).

■ s.63(7A) and (7B) CJPOA 1994 inserted by s.58(6)
ASBA means that a person commits an offence if
s/he:

  • Knows that a direction to leave which applies to
    her/him has been give and
  • Makes preparations for or attends a gathering to
    which s.63 applies (i.e. indoor or outdoor rave)
    within 24 hours of the start of that direction

Aggravated Trespass [s.59 ASBA 2003]

- S.59 ASBA 2003 amends ss.68 and s.69 of CJPOA 1994 to extend provisions relating to the offence of aggravated trespass to cover trespass in buildings, as well as in the open air.

  NB. This means that an offence of aggravated trespass will be committed where a person trespassing, in a building or in the open air, does anything which is intended to intimidate or deter persons from engaging in a lawful activity, or to obstruct or disrupt that activity.

Powers to Remove Trespassers: Alternative Site Available [s.60 ASBA 2003]

- If the senior police officer present at a scene reasonably believes that the conditions in s.60(2) (described below) are satisfied in relation to a person and land, s/he may direct the person to:

  - Leave the land
  - Remove any vehicle and other property s/he has with her/him on the land

- The conditions contained are that:

  - The person and 1 or more others (the trespassers) are trespassing on the land
  - The trespassers have between them at least 1 vehicle on the land

- The trespassers are present on the land with the common purpose of residing there for any period
- It appears to the officer that the person has 1 or more caravans in her/his possession or control on the land, that there is a suitable pitch on a relevant caravan site for that caravan or each of those caravans
- The occupier of the land or a person acting on her/his behalf has asked the police to remove the trespassers from the land [s.60(2) CJPOA 1994 as inserted by s.60 ASBA 2003]

■ A direction under s.60 (1) CJPOA 1994 may be communicated to the person to whom it applies by any constable at the scene [s.60 (3) CJPOA 1994 as inserted by s.60 ASBA 2003].

■ The police officer must consult every local authority within whose area the land is situated as to whether there is a suitable pitch for the caravan/s on a resident site situated in the local authority area **if**:

- S/he proposes to give a direction under s.60(1) CJPOA 1994 and
- It appears to her/him that the person has 1 or more caravans in her/his possession or under her/his control on the land [s.60(4);(5) CJPOA 1994 as inserted by s.60 ASBA 2003]

Offences [ss.61; 62 ASBA 2003]

■ S.61 ASBA 2003 inserts s.62B into the CJPOA 1994 (failure to comply with direction under s.62A: offences).

- A person commits an offence if s/he knows that a direction under s.62A(1) has been given which applies to her/him and

  - S/he fails to leave the relevant land as soon as reasonably practicable or
  - Enters any land in the area of the relevant local authority as a trespasser with the intention of residing there before the end of 3 months from the day the direction was given [s.62B(1); (2) CJPOA 1994 inserted by s.61 ASBA 2003]

- A person guilty of an offence under s.62A is liable on summary conviction to imprisonment for a term not exceeding 3 months or a fine not exceeding level 4 on the standard scale or both [s.62B(3) CJPOA 1994].

  NB. A constable in uniform who reasonably suspects a person is committing an offence under s.62B may arrest her/him without a warrant [s.62B (4) CJPOA 1994].

- In proceedings for an offence under s.61, it is a defence for the accused to show that:

  - S/he was not trespassing on the land in question or that
  - S/he had a reasonable excuse for failing to leave it the relevant land as soon as reasonably practicable or for entering land in the area of the relevant local authority as trespasser with the intention of residing there or

- At the time the direction was given, s/he was under the age of 18 and was residing with her/his parent/guardian [s.61 (5) ASBA 2003].

■ S.62 ASBA 2003 inserts s.62C into the CJPOA 1994 (failure to comply with directions under s.62A: seizure).

■ A constable may seize and remove the vehicle if a direction has been given under s.62A(1) CJPOA 1994 and s/he reasonably suspects that a person to whom the direction applies has, without reasonable excuse:

- Failed to remove any vehicle on the relevant land which appears to the constable to belong to that person or to be in her/his possession or under her/his control
- Entered any land in the area of the relevant local authority as a trespasser with a vehicle before the end of 3 months from the day the direction is given [s.62C(1),(2) CJPOA 1994 inserted by s.62 ASBA 2003]

Part 8: High Hedges

Summary of Provisions

- Local authorities now have powers to deal with complaints about high hedges which are having an adverse effect on a neighbour's enjoyment of her/his property.

- Complaining to a local authority should be a last resort and the local authority is able to charge a fee for this service.

- If the local authority considers the circumstances justify it, it can issue a formal notice outlining what formal action should be taken to remedy the problem and to prevent it recurring.

- Failure to comply with the notice will be an offence.

- The local authority also has powers to undertake the work itself and recover the costs from the owners of the hedge.

Part 9: Miscellaneous Powers

Anti-social Behaviour Orders (ASBOs) [s.1; 1A CDA 1998 as amended by s.85 ASBA 2003]

■ An application for an order under this section may be made by a relevant authority i.e. the council for a local government area, (in England) County Council, any chief officer of police for the area, chief constable of British Transport Police Force, any person registered as a social landlord or a housing action trust if it appears to them that the conditions described below are fulfilled with respect to any person aged 10 or over [s.1(1A) CDA 1998 as amended by s.61(1) PRA 2002 and s.85 ASBA 2003]

NB. The Secretary of State now has the power to enable non-Home Office police forces to apply for Anti-social Behaviour Orders [s.1A as inserted by s.62 PRA 2002].

Conditions [s.1 (1) (a) & (b) CDA 1998 as amended by s.61 (2) PRA 2002]

■ The conditions are that:

• The person has, since the section's commencement on 01.04.99 [SI 1998/3263] acted in an anti-social manner i.e. a manner that caused or was likely to cause harassment, alarm or distress to one or more persons not of the same household as her/himself **and**

- Such an order is necessary to protect 'relevant' persons in the local government area in which the harassment, alarm or distress was caused or was likely to be caused; in the police area or area policed by the British Transport police, or premises provided or managed by the social landlord, from further anti-social acts by her/him.

■ Such an application must be made by complaint to the magistrates' court whose commission area includes the local government or police area concerned [s.1 (3) CDA 1998 as amended by s.61 (6) PRA 2002 and s.85(3) ASBA 2003].

■ If on application, it is proved that the conditions mentioned in s.1 (1) are fulfilled the magistrates' court may make an 'Anti-social Behaviour Order' (ASBO) under this section [s.1 (4) CDA 1998].

NB. For the purposes of determining whether the 'anti-social manner' criterion of s.1 (1) (a) is satisfied the court must disregard any act of the defendant which s/he shows was reasonable in the circumstances [s.1 (5) CDA 1998].

s.1B CDA 1998 introduced by s.63 PRA 2002 enables relevant authorities to apply to the County Court in certain circumstances for an ASBO.

Effect of Anti-social Behaviour Order [s.1 (4) & (6) as substituted by s.61 (7) PRA 2002]

- The above order prohibits the defendant from doing anything described in the order.

- Prohibitions are those necessary for the purpose of protecting from further anti-social acts by defendant, relevant persons elsewhere in England and Wales.

Consultation Requirements [s.1E CDA 1998 as inserted by s.66 PRA 2002]

- A council of a local government area must consult the chief officer of police with jurisdiction in that area before applying for an ASBO.

- Similarly, a chief officer of police must consult the council of the local government area before s/he initiates an application.

- British Transport police and registered social landlords must consult both the appropriate council and police.

Interim Orders [s.1D CDA 1998 as inserted by s.65 PRA 2002]

- A magistrates' court or the County Court is able to make an interim order under s.1 or new s.1B before the application process is complete, if the court considers it just to do so [s.1D(1) CDA 1998].

NB. Interim orders are not available to criminal courts because orders under s.1C (see below) can only be made in the criminal courts once the case is complete and the offender has been convicted.

Duration of Anti-social Behaviour Order [s.1 (7) CDA 1998]

■ The order will have effect for a period not less than 2 years which is specified in the order, or until further order is made.

Variation or Discharge of Anti-social Behaviour (including interim) Order [s.1 (8) & (9) CDA 1998]

■ Except by the consent of both parties, no ASBO will be discharged before the end of the 2 years beginning with the date of its service [s.1 (9) CDA 1998].

NB. The consent provision does not apply to an order under s.1C in criminal proceedings (see below).

■ The applicant or the defendant may apply by complaint to the court which made an ASBO for it to be varied or discharged by a further order [s.1 (8) CDA 1998].

Breach of Anti-social Behaviour (including interim) Order [s.1 (10) & (11) CDA 1998 as amended]

■ If, without reasonable excuse a person does anything which s/he is prohibited from doing by an ASBO, s/he is guilty of an offence and liable:

- On summary conviction, to imprisonment for up to 6 months or a fine not exceeding the statutory maximum, or both
- On conviction on indictment, to imprisonment for up to 5 years or a fine [s.1 (10)]

NB. A person convicted of such a breach cannot be given a conditional discharge under s.12 PCCSA 2000 [s.1 (11) CDA 1998].

Appeal against Anti-social Behaviour (including interim) Order [s.4 CDA 1998]

■ An appeal against an ASBO made by the magistrates' court will be heard by the Crown Court.

■ On such an appeal, the Crown Court may:

- Make such orders as may be necessary to give effect to its determination of the appeal and
- Also make such incidental or consequential orders as appear to it to be just

NB. Any order of the Crown Court made on an appeal under s.4 CDA 1998 (other than one directing an application be re-heard by the magistrates' court) must, for purposes of future variation or discharge applications be treated as if an order of the magistrates' court from which appeal was brought and not an order of the Crown Court.

If an ASBO is made in respect of a person aged under 16, the court which makes the order must make a Parenting Order if it is satisfied that the relevant condition is fulfilled or if it is not so satisfied, must state in open court that it is not and why it is not [s. 9(1B) CDA 1998] – see also CAE's companion guide to the Crime and Disorder Act 1998.

Certain Orders Made on Conviction in Criminal Proceedings [s.1C CDA 1998 as inserted by s.64 PRA 2002]

■ Where a person has been convicted of a 'relevant offence' (i.e. an offence committed on or after 02.12.02) and the court considers an offender has acted, at any time since the commencement date, in an anti-social manner, and an order under this section is necessary to protect persons in England or Wales from further anti-social acts, it may make an order which prohibits the offender from doing anything described in that order [s.1C CDA 1998 inserted by s.64 PRA 2002 and amended by s.86 ASBA 2003].

NB. The court may make an order if the prosecutor asks it to do so or if the court thinks it appropriate. An order under this provision may be made only in addition to any sentence imposed [s.1C (4) CDA 1998 amended by s.86 (1) ASBA 2003]. An offender subject to an order under s.1C may apply to the court which made it for it to be varied or discharged.)

Lifting of Automatic Reporting Restrictions [s.86 (3) ASBA 2003]

■ For breaches of an ASBO imposed on a child/young person convicted of an offence, restrictions on reports of such proceedings imposed by s.49 CYPA 1933 are lifted and s.39 of that Act (powers to prohibit publication of certain matter) applies and provides the court with discretion.

Penalty Notices for Disorderly Behaviour By Young Person [s. 2(1) CJPA 2001]

■ A constable who has reason to believe a person aged 16 or over has committed a penalty offence may give her/him a Penalty Notice in respect of the offence [s.2(1) CJPA 2001 as amended by s.87 ASBA 2003].

NB. A 'Penalty Notice' means a notice offering the opportunity to discharge any liability to be convicted of the offence by paying a penalty [s.2 (4) CJPA 2001].

The Secretary of State may introduce by order, an age limit between 10 and 16 and specify that for such a person, her/his parent or guardian is to be notified of the giving of the notice and become liable for payment of the penalty [s.2(6)CJPA 2001 introduced by s.87(3) ASBA 2003].

Curfew Orders and Supervision Orders

- Schedule 2 (Curfew Orders and Supervision Orders under the Powers of Criminal Courts (Sentencing) Act 2000 applies as described below [s.88 ASBA 2003]

- Where a person is convicted, the court may (subject to restrictions in ss.34–36 PCCSA 2000) make an order requiring her/him to remain for periods specified at a specified place [s.37(1) PCCSA 2000].

- A Curfew Order may specify different places or periods for different days but must not specify periods:

  - Beyond 6 months of order being made or
  - Which amount to less than 2 or more than 12 hours in any day [s.37(3) PCCSA 2000]

  NB. Requirements shall as far as practicable avoid any conflict with offender's religious beliefs, requirements of any other Community Order to which s/he may be subject and any interference with times, if any, at which s/he normally works or attends school [s.37(5) PCCSA 2000].

- A court cannot make a Curfew Order unless notified by Secretary of State arrangements for monitoring offenders' whereabouts are available and notification has not been withdrawn [s.37(7) PCCSA 2000] (all forms of curfew are now available throughout England and Wales).

■ Before making a Curfew Order the court must obtain and consider information about the place proposed to be specified (including information as to attitude of persons likely to be affected by the enforced presence of the offender there) [s.37(8) PCCSA 2000].

■ Before making a Curfew Order in respect of an offender aged under 16, the court must obtain and consider information about her/his family circumstances and the likely affect of such an order on these circumstances [s.37(9) PCCSA 2000].

■ Before making a Curfew Order the court must explain to the offender in ordinary language:

• The effect of the order (including any additional requirements such as electronic monitoring)
• The consequences which may follow under Part II of Sch.3 to the PCCSA 2000 if s/he fails to comply with any requirements of the Order and
• That court has power under Parts III and IV of Sch.3 to review order on application of offender or responsible officer [s.37(10) PCCSA 2000]

NB. Where a court has been notified necessary arrangements had been made in relevant area it is able to include requirements for securing electronic monitoring of offender's whereabouts during the curfew periods specified [s.36B(1) PCCSA 2000 introduced by s.52 CJCSA 2000].

Failure to Comply & Revocation and Amendment [s.39 & Sch.3 PCCSA 2000]

■ If at any time while a Curfew Order is in force in respect of an offender it appears on information to a JP acting for the petty sessions area concerned that the offender has failed to comply with any of the order's requirements, s/he may issue a summons, or if the information is in writing on oath, issue a warrant for the offender's arrest [Sch.3 para.3 (1) PCCSA 2000].

■ If proved to the satisfaction of a magistrates' court before which an offender appears/is brought that s/he has failed without reasonable cause to comply with any requirements of the relevant order, the court may:

- Impose a fine of up to £1,000
- Where the offender is 16 or over (subject to para.7) make a Community Punishment Order in respect of her/him
- Where the offender is less than 16 it may (subject to para.8) make an Attendance Centre Order
- Where the relevant order was made by a magistrates' court, it may deal with her/him for the offence in respect of which the order was made in any way it could have dealt with her/him if s/he had just been convicted by the court of the offence [Sch.3 para.4 PCCSA 2000]

Supervision Orders [s.63 & Sch.6 PCCSA 2000]

Criteria

■ Where a child/young person is convicted of an offence and the court is satisfied that s/he resides/will reside in the area of the local authority, it may place her/him under the supervision of:

- The local authority designated by the order
- A probation officer
- A member of the YOT

■ The above officer must advice, assist and befriend the offender [ss.63 (1); 64(4) PCCSA 2000].

NB. The court must not designate a local authority as supervisor unless that local authority agrees or it appears that the offender does or will reside in that authority's area. [s.64 (5) PCCSA 2000].

Duration

■ A Supervision Order, unless revoked or specified for a shorter period will last 3 years from the date it is made [s.63 (7) PCCSA 2000].

NB. Nothing in the PCCSA 2000 prevents a court which makes a Supervision Order also making a Curfew Order with respect to the offender [s.64A introduced by Sch.2 para. 3 ASBA 2003].

**Requirements to Comply With Directions of
Supervisor/ Live With A Named Individual**

■ A Supervision Order may (assuming that the court is
satisfied there is a local authority scheme as per s.66
PCCSA 2000) require the offender to comply with
directions of the supervisor requiring any or all of
the following, to:

  • Live at place/s specified for specified period/s
    of time
  • Present her/himself to person/s specified in
    the directions at place/s and on day/s specified
  • Participate in specified activities on specified
    days [Sch.6 para.2(2) PCCSA 2000]

■ With respect to a young person of 14 or over who
consents, a court is empowered to impose drug
treatment/testing requirements [Sch.6 para. 6A
PCCSA 2000 introduced by Sch.24 CJA 2003]

■ The total number of days in respect of which an
offender may be required to comply with such
directions must not exceed 180, or fewer if so
specified in the Supervision Order [Sch.6 para.2(5)
PCCSA 2000 as amended by Sch.2 para.4 ASBA
2003].

*NB. Any day on which directions given were not
complied with does not count toward the total
allowable [Sch.3 para. 2(6) PCCSA 2000]. These
arrangements are to be piloted in autumn 2004.*

■ A Supervision Order may also require an offender to reside with a named individual (who agrees to the requirement) so long as this is consistent with other more general requirements of the supervising officer [Sch.6 para.1 PCCSA 2000].

Requirements as to Activities, Reparation

■ Unless the Supervision Order requires the offender to comply with directions given by the supervisor under Sch.6 para.2(1) PCCSA 2000 (see above), it may for a maximum of 180 days require the offender to:

- Live at specified place/s for specified period/s
- Present her/himself to specified person/s at specified place/s on specified day/s
- Participate in specified activities on day/s so specified
- Make reparation specified in the order to person/s specified and/or to the community at large
- Refrain from participating in activities specified in the order on specified day/s or for a portion or all of the period of the Supervision Order [Sch.6 para.3 PCCSA 2000 as amended by Sch.2 para.3 ASBA 2003]

NB. Reparation = reparation for the offence other than by payment of compensation. These arrangements are to be piloted in autumn 2004.

Requirements to Live For Specified Period in Local Authority Accommodation [Sch.6 para.5 PCCSA 2000]

- Where the following conditions are satisfied, a Supervision Order may impose for a maximum of 6 months a 'Local Authority Residence Requirement' which compels the offender to live for a specified period in local authority accommodation:

  - A Supervision Order has previously been made with respect to the offender
  - That Supervision Order imposed requirements (other than one for treatment for a mental condition) or a 'Local Authority Requirement' with which the offender has failed to comply or
  - The offender was convicted of an offence whilst that order was in force and
  - The court is satisfied that the failure to comply or the behaviour which constituted the offence was due to a significant extent to the circumstances in which the offender was living (not applicable if the offender already in local authority accommodation) and
  - That imposition of a Local Authority Residence Requirement will assist in her/his rehabilitation.

  NB. The court must consult the designated local authority before imposing the residence requirement [Sch.6 para.5 (4) PCCSA 2000].

- Further potential requirements for treatment for mental conditions and for education are provided for in Sch.6 paras.6–7 PCCSA 2000.

**Requirement to Live for a Specified Period
in with Local Authority Foster Parent
[Sch.6 para. 5A PCCSA 2000 inserted by
Sch.2 para.4 ASBA 2003]**

*NB. Fostering as part of a Supervision Order is to be
piloted from autumn 2004.*

- A Supervision order may impose a 'Foster Parent
Residence Requirement 'that the offender must live
for a specified period with a local authority foster
parent, if the:

  - Offence is punishable with imprisonment
  in the case of an offender aged 18 or over
  - Offence, or combination of it and one or
  more associated offences, was so serious
  that a custodial sentence would normally be
  appropriate (or in the case of a 10 or 11 year
  old child, would be so if the offender were
  12 or over) **and**
  - Court is satisfied that the behaviour which
  constituted the offence was due to a significant
  extent to the circumstances in which the
  offender was living and that imposition of
  the requirement will assist rehabilitation

- A Foster Parent Residence Requirement must
designate the local authority which is to place the
offender under s.23 (2) (a) CA 1989 which will be
the authority in which the offender resides.

- A court cannot impose a residence requirement
unless notified by the Secretary of state that

arrangements are in place and unless it has consulted the designated local authority.

NB. Unless extended as a result of a breach, the maximum period is 12 months.

Breach/ Revocation & Amendment
[Sch.7 para.2 PCCSA 2000 as amended]

■ If the court is satisfied on the application of the supervisor that an offender has failed to comply with any requirements it may (whether or not it revokes or amends the Supervision Order):

- Fine the offender up to £1,000
- Impose a Curfew Order (unless offender is already subject to a Curfew Order)
- Impose an Attendance Centre Order
- (If the Supervision Order was made by a magistrates' court), revoke it and deal with the offence in any way which had been available when the order was made
- (If the Supervision Order was made by the Crown Court), commit the offender in custody or release on bail until s/he can be brought or appear before the Crown Court.

■ In relation to a Supervision Order imposing a Foster Parent Residence Requirement, the court may extend the period specified in the requirement to a period of not more than 18 months beginning on which the requirement first took effect [Sch.7 para.5(2A) PCCSA 2000 inserted by Sch.2 para. 4 ASBA 2003]

NB. The court must take into account the extent to which the offender has complied with the requirements of the Supervision Order [Sch.7 para.2 (7) PCCSA 2000].

■ On the application of supervisor or offender (or parent on behalf of a child/young person), the court may revoke or amend the Supervision Order by cancelling any requirement in it or inserting any provision which could have been included [Sch.7 para.5 PCCSA 2000].

NB. Sch.7 PCCSA 2000 contains further restrictions on the court's powers to revoke/amend Supervision Orders.

Extension of Powers of Community Support Officers etc [s.89 ASBA 2003]

■ S.89 extends the powers of community support officers (CSOs) contained in part 1 Sch.4 PRA 2002 with the following consequences.

Fixed Penalty Notice

■ A CSO may, in relation to any individual who s/he has reason to believe has committed a relevant fixed penalty offence at a place within the relevant police area, issue a Fixed Penalty Notice

■ Those powers in respect of a relevant fixed penalty offence are as follows:

  • The powers of a constable in uniform and of an authorised constable to give a Penalty Notice under Chapter 1 of Part 1 Criminal Justice and Police Act 2001 (Fixed Penalty Notices in respect of offences of disorder)

  • The power of a constable in uniform to give a person a Fixed Penalty Notice under s.54 Road Traffic Offenders Act 1988 (Fixed Penalty Notices) in respect of an offence under s.72 of the Highway Act 1835 (riding on a footway) committed by cycling

NB. A community support officers (CSO) also has the power of a constable in uniform under s.163 (2)

Road Traffic Act 1968 to **stop** *a cycle but only if s/he has reason to believe that the rider has committed an offence under s.72 Highways Act 1835 (riding on a footway) by cycling [para.11A Sch.4 PRA 2002 inserted by s.89 (3) ASBA 2003].*

- The power of an authorised officer of a local authority to give a notice under s.4 Dogs (Fouling of Land) Act 1996 (Fixed Penalty Notices in respect of dog fouling) and
- The power of an authorised officer of a litter authority to give a notice under s.88 Environmental Protection Act 1990 (Fixed Penalty Notices in respect of litter)

■ A CSO who has reason to believe that another person has committed a relevant offence or is acting in an anti-social manner in the relevant police area, may require that other person to offer her/his name and address, and is also empowered to require the other person to wait with her/him, for a period not exceeding 30 minutes, for the arrival of a constable **if**:

- The other person fails to comply with the requirement, or
- The CSO has reasonable grounds for suspecting the other person has provided a name or address that is false or inaccurate,

NB. A person who has been required to wait with a CSO may elect that (instead of waiting) s/he will accompany the CSO to a police station in the relevant police area.

■ A person who fails to comply with a requirement to provide her/his name and address, makes off while subject to a requirement to await the arrival of constable or makes off while accompanying a person to a police station:

• Is guilty of an offence and is be liable, on summary conviction, to a fine not exceeding level 3 on the standard scale

Alcohol Consumption in Designated Public Places

■ A CSO also has, within the relevant police area, the powers of a constable under s.12 Criminal Justice and Police Act 2001 (alcohol consumption in public places) substituted by the Licensing Act 2003 Sch.6 to:

• Impose a requirement under sub-section 12 (2) not to consume alcohol in a designated public place
• Dispose under sub-section 12(3) of anything surrendered to her/him

Confiscation of Alcohol

■ A CSO also has, within the relevant police area, the powers of a constable under s. 1 Confiscation of Alcohol (Young Persons) Act 1997 (confiscation of alcohol) to:

• Impose a requirement under sub-section 1(1)
• Dispose under sub-section 1(2) of anything surrendered to her/him

Confiscation of Tobacco

■ A CSO has, within the relevant police area power to:

- Seize anything a constable in uniform has a duty to seize under s.7 (3) Children and Young Persons Act 1933 (seizure of tobacco etc from young persons) and
- Dispose of anything that a constable may dispose of under that sub-section and
- Dispose of anything in such manner as the police authority may direct

Entry to Save Life or Limb or Prevent Serious Damage to Property

■ A CSO has the powers of a constable under s.17 PACE 1984 Act to enter and search any premises in the relevant police area for the purpose of saving life or limb or preventing serious damage to property.

Seizure of Vehicles Used to Cause Alarm etc

■ A CSO within the relevant police area, has all the powers of a uniformed constable under s.59(3) PRA 2002

NB. A person to whom this paragraph applies shall not enter any premises in exercise of the power conferred by section 59(3)(c) except in the company, and under the supervision, of a constable.

Abandoned Vehicles

■ A CSO in the relevant police area may exercise
powers made by regulations under s. 99 of
Road Traffic Regulation Act 1984 (removal of
abandoned vehicles).

Power to Stop Vehicle for Testing

■ A CSO within the relevant police area, has the power
of a constable in uniform to stop a vehicle under
s.67 (3) Road Traffic Act 1988 for the purposes
of a test under subsection (1) of that section.

A Power to Control Traffic for Purposes of Escorting a Load of Exceptional Dimensions

■ A CSO has, for the purpose of escorting a vehicle
or trailer carrying a load of exceptional dimensions
either to or from the relevant police area, the power
of a constable engaged in the regulation of traffic
in a road, to:

- Direct a vehicle to stop
- Make a vehicle proceed in, or keep to,
a particular line of traffic and
- Direct pedestrians to stop

*NB. For the purpose of an offence under the Road
Traffic Act 1988 of failing to comply with directions
of a constable engaged in regulation of traffic
in a road, a CSO is to be considered equivalent
to a constable.*

Carrying Out of Road Checks

■ A CSO in the relevant police area has:

- The power to carry out any road check, the carrying out of which by a police officer is authorised under s. 4 of the Police and Criminal Evidence Act 1984 Act (road checks)
- For the purpose of exercising that power, the power conferred by s.163 Road Traffic Act 1988 (power of police to stop vehicles) on a constable in uniform to stop a vehicle

Cordoned Areas

■ A CSO has, in relation to any cordoned area in the relevant police area, all the powers of a constable in uniform under s. 36 Terrorism Act 2000 (enforcement of cordoned area) to give orders, make arrangements or impose prohibitions or restrictions.

Power to Stop and Search Vehicles etc. in Authorised Areas

■ A CSO has, in any authorised area within the relevant police area, all the powers of a constable in uniform by virtue of s. 44(1)(a) and (d) and (2)(b) and 45(2) Terrorism Act 2000 (powers of stop and search) to:

- Stop and search vehicles
- Search anything in or on a vehicle or anything carried by the driver of a vehicle or any passenger in a vehicle

- Search anything carried by a pedestrian and
- Seize and retain any article discovered in the course of a search carried out by her/him or by a constable by virtue of any provision of s.44(1) or (2) TA 2000

NB. A CSO shall not exercise any power of stop, search or seizure except in the company, and under the supervision, of a constable.

Report by Local Authority in Certain Cases Where Person is Remanded on Bail [s.90 ASBA 2003]

■ The court may (in the case of a 10 or 11 year old on bail) order a local authority to make an oral or written report (within a specified period not exceeding 7 days) specifying where the person is likely to be placed or maintained if s/he is further remanded to local authority accommodation if either:

- The person is charged with or has been convicted of a serious offence or
- In the opinion of the court, the person is a persistent offender [s.23B (1); (2); (4) introduced by s.90 ASBA 2003]

■ Such an order must designate the local authority which is to make the report and that must be the authority the court would have designated under s.23 (2) CYPA 1969 if the person had been remanded to local authority accommodation [s.23B(3) CYPA 1969].

NB. A 'serious offence' means an offence punishable in the case of an adult with imprisonment for term of 2 years or more [s.23B(7) CYPA 1969]

If the Secretary of State orders it, the above provisions will also apply to 12–16 year olds inclusive, the requirements of s.23AA (3) (electronic monitoring) are fulfilled and, where a person is remanded after conviction, the court is satisfied that the behaviour constituting the offence was due, to a significant extent, to the circumstances in which the offender was living [s.23B (6) CYPA 1969 as inserted by s.90 (7) ASBA 2003].

Other Legislation Relevant to Anti-social Behaviours

Motorised Scooters

■ Motorised scooters e.g. a 'Goped' are designed for off-road use only.

■ To be used legally on the road, a category P, A or B licence would be required (minimum age 16) and the scooter itself would have to be modified to meet all the requirements of the RTA 1968 and associated regulations.

Fireworks [Fireworks Act 2003 & Fireworks Regulations 2004]

■ It is an offence to contravene the Fireworks Regulations 2004 SI 2004/1836 [s.1 Fireworks Act 2003].

■ Under 18 year olds may not (subject to certain exceptions relating to employment or business covered in reg. 6) possess 'adult fireworks' (defined in reg.3) in public places [regulation 4 Fireworks Regulations 2004].

■ No person may use an adult firework during night hours except:

• During 'permitted fireworks nights' or
• By any person employed by a local authority and who use the firework in question for the

purposes of a local authority display or at a national public celebration or national commemorative event [reg.7 Fireworks Regulations 2004]

■ 'Night hours' are the period from 11pm to 7am the following day and a permitted fireworks night means a period beginning at 11pm on:

- The first day of the Chinese New Year and ending at 1am the following day
- 5th November and ending at 12am the following day
- The day of Diwali and ending at 1am the following day
- 31st December and ending at 1am the following day [reg.7(3) Fireworks Regulations 2004]

Blades/ Knives

■ s. 1 Offensive Weapons Act 1996 amended s.24 Police and Criminal Evidence Act 1984 to make the following offences arrestable:

- s. 1(1) Prevention of Crime Act 1953 (prohibition of the carrying of offensive weapons without lawful authority or reasonable excuse)
- s. 139(1) Criminal Justice Act 1988 (offence of having article with blade or point in public place)
- s.139A (1) or (2) Criminal Justice Act 1988 (offence of having article with blade or point (or offensive weapon) on school premises)

NB. The Criminal Justice Act 1988 (Offensive Weapons) (Amendment) Order 2004 amends the Schedule to the Criminal Justice Act 1988 (Offensive Weapons) Order 1988 which specifies offensive weapons for the purposes of s.141 Criminal Justice Act 1988),by adding a stealth knife i.e. a knife or spike, which has a blade, or sharp point, made from a material that is not readily detectable by apparatus used for detecting metal and which is not designed for domestic use or for use in the processing, preparation or consumption of food or as a toy; a straight, side-handled or friction-lock truncheon (sometimes known as a baton).

Subject Index

Appendix: CAE Publications

- Personal Guides:
  - Children Act 1989 in the Context of the Human Rights Act 1998
  - Childminding and Day Care (England)
  - Child Protection
  - Residential Care of Children
  - Fostering
  - 'How Old Do I Have To Be...?' (simple guide to the rights and responsibilities of 0–21 year olds)
  - Domestic Violence
  - Looking After Children: Good Parenting, Good Outcomes (DH LAC System)
  - Crime and Disorder Act 1998
  - Sexual Offences Act 2003
  - Anti-social Behaviour

Planned for publication in early 2005
The Children Act 2004

All available from: Children Act Enterprises Ltd,
103 Mayfield Road, South Croydon, Surrey CR2 0BH
tel: 020 8651 0554 fax: 020 8405 8483
email: childact@dial.pipex.com

www.caeuk.org

Discounts for orders of 50 or more of any one title